Copyright

Contents

Introduction

An affiliate is similar to an online sales representative. An affiliate's job is to promote and sell products from vendors. Affiliates are compensated in the form of commissions on each sale. It's a low-cost business that can generate a lot of money if done correctly.

One of the many marvels of the Internet business is that it gives everyone the same chance to succeed. One of these businesses is affiliate marketing. Creativity and skills are what distinguishes a successful online entrepreneur from the rest.

This book will teach you how to succeed. It will go over in depth techniques that you can add to your marketing arsenal. You will be exposed to new perspectives on the business, and you will learn what others have learned through years of trial and error.

An affiliate can be done by anyone. All you

need is a computer with a good Internet connection and a little bit of IT knowledge, and you're ready to go. But, of course, you'd want to take it a step further with this course.

Affiliate Marketing's Benefits and Drawbacks

For those who are still unsure whether affiliate marketing is still significant and in demand, the answer is yes.

It has gone through many changes in the last few years, as well as ups and downs. Some methods and websites have become obsolete as a result of the passage of time. It has, in essence, evolved. It will continue to evolve and become more significant. It has proven to be an important part of the advancement of online marketing.

Let's address the concerns that a newcomer may still have about affiliate marketing. Affiliate marketing has been shown to benefit all parties involved in a transaction. Here are the advantages and disadvantages for your consideration.

Pros

Regarding the Product Vendor

If you look at affiliate marketing through the eyes of a product vendor, you'll see that it's a great deal. A vendor is not required to pay any fees upfront for affiliates to begin promoting their product, and affiliates are compensated based on their performance.

As a result, a vendor does not have to be concerned about a loss of investment because if the affiliate does not perform, the vendor does not have to pay. As previously stated, the affiliate business is based on commissions.

And the affiliates are sent out to promote the product for little risk and almost no cost. They also put in a lot of effort for their own benefit.

For the Client

A product that the customer has been looking for will be delivered to them via an affiliate. Remember that an affiliate will go out of his way to sell a product, so they will typically provide product details for the customer's benefit.

Successful affiliates typically post a product review on their own website for customers to read. All of the functions, features, and weaknesses of the products are addressed here. This, of course, makes it easier for the customer to determine whether or not this product is right for them.

Some affiliates also offer bonuses to customers who buy from them.

These bonuses are not a necessary part of an affiliate business, but those affiliates who want to make a lot of money will do it. And, once again, the customers benefit from this.

Regarding The Affiliate

As previously stated, the affiliate benefits from this business by earning extra money for doing something simple. And, if done correctly, affiliates would gain far more than just "extra money." As an affiliate, they could run a profitable business.

If the affiliate is truly serious about the online business and devotes themselves to it, they may be able to learn to become product vendors themselves one day. Of course, this is entirely up to them. They could simply remain an affiliate and expand their own reach if they so desire.

<u>**Cons**</u>

Regarding the Product Vendor

Some affiliates, motivated solely by the desire to make a sale, would use false advertising to sell their products. They would sell the product for more than it is worth, or they might promise things that the product cannot deliver.

This is something that the vendor does not have complete control over, especially for products or promotions involving a large number of affiliates. They can monitor the affiliates' advertising habits, but not all of them, because that would take a lot of energy.

When a customer is dissatisfied with a product that does not deliver what was falsely promised, they will request a refund. Having a large number of refunds will seriously harm the business.

The harm caused by false advertising is far more dangerous than simply issuing refunds. The vendor's credibility will suffer as a result. Their reputation will be tarnished, and they will be regarded as con artists.

Regarding The Affiliate

The swindling game can be played both ways. If an unlucky affiliate participates in a program with a dishonest vendor, they will suffer losses.

Typically, these vendors would launch an affiliate program and assign affiliates to make promotions and sales. Then, once everything is completed, they close their business, leaving the affiliates with no commission for all sales made.

It's difficult to spot these dishonest vendors. Knowing them would necessitate prior experience. To avoid these types of vendors, this business must be conducted with vigilance and caution.

Conclusion

Everything has advantages and disadvantages. And there will be dishonest people who take advantage of a profitable and significant business like affiliate marketing.

These are the obstacles we must overcome (or avoid, in the case of swindlers) in order to succeed. Even though it's a great way to supplement your income, it's also risky. But, given the potential of this particular business, all of the effort will be worthwhile.

Selecting the Most Profitable Product to Promote

There are two ways to work as an affiliate:

1) You can take whatever you can get your hands on and work extremely hard, or

2) You can select the best products that generate the highest profits.

Of course, being a prolific affiliate with achievements and a work rate that outperforms others is always a plus. But, are all products worthwhile of your time and effort?

A new affiliate will always participate in as many affiliate programs as they can. This is due to the fact that a novice is always hungry. However, how long can you continue to work in this manner? You'll be exhausted one day, and your subscribers will be exhausted as well.

So, choosing the best products is the best way to overcome exhaustion while still earning high commissions. In this context, the best products are those that can guarantee you high earnings as an affiliate.

Before deciding on a product to promote, there are a few factors to consider. To be considered a good product for you, a product must meet certain criteria. However, determining the quality of the product will not be difficult.

You might think that by doing this, you'll be limiting your options and, as a result, your earning potential as an affiliate. In reality, you don't lose much and have a lot more to gain.

This is due to the fact that a new product is released every day. You will never run out of products to promote, so you won't lose anything if you cherry-pick. If you miss an opportunity (for example, a bestselling product), you can always move on to the next one.

Commissions and earnings, on the other hand, should not be taken lightly. You must ensure that you obtain the best product to promote. So, what are the requirements for a good product to be promoted?

Product Selection Criteria

The commission should be high. When

selecting a product, ensure that the provided commission rate is not less than 50% if it is not a high-ticket sale.

A typical commission rate for a low-ticket item is 50% or higher. It can even reach 100 percent. Yes, the affiliate is entitled to keep the entire proceeds from the sale of the product.

When it comes to high-ticket items, however, the commission can be less than 50%. For example, the commission on a $997 product would be $197. However, because it is high-priced, despite having a lower commission percentage, it is still high in value.

Selling high-ticket items is more difficult than selling low-ticket items. The conversion rate is significantly lower. You must first build your list and credentials before taking on the high-ticket challenges.

Here's a comparison of selling high and low ticket items:

- Low ticket product – with a $34 product, your sales can easily reach 400 or more, and you've made $13,600 or more.

- High ticket product – selling high priced product is more difficult; if you can only make 10 copies of sales, you earn only $9,970.

This is the distinction between selecting a low tick or a high tick product.

Digital Product

There are numerous affiliate programs from which to choose. Online, you can sell and promote appliances, books, clothing, and a variety of other items. However, the best products, those that sell the most, are digital products.

Physical products not only do not sell as well as digital products, but they also offer lower commission rates. To make enough money from commissions on physical products, massive conversion rates would be required.

Among the digital products are:

- Software

- E-Books

- Webinars

- Video Instructions

Every day, new digital products are released, and their sales can reach thousands of dollars. There's no need to be concerned about a lack of products to promote.

Physical products would also complicate delivery. If you were an affiliate who connected a buyer to a vendor and they were both from different countries, the shipment could go wrong. And if the customer requests a refund, your commission is forfeited.

There will be occasions when a customer requests a refund when purchasing digital products, but this is a very rare occurrence.

Furthermore, digital products require only a few simple steps to download the file in PDF format, and you can start enjoying the product almost immediately; in contrast, a physical book requires shipment, which can take months.

Furthermore, with digital products, there will be no shipping issues. One less thing to be concerned about!

Product High Quality

First and foremost, you should be aware of the product's quality. You must first ensure that it is a product worth purchasing for you before you can determine whether it is a product worth selling.

You don't want to sell subpar products because they will not only fail, but they will also harm your credibility as an affiliate.

You may lose the trust of your subscribers. That is not desirable because your email list and subscribers are an important part of your business.

Avoid upsetting them at all costs, as they can unsubscribe you just as easily as they can subscribe to you.

Tip: If you're not sure about purchasing the product, do some research on the reviews articles written by other users about the product you've chosen.

You can also look at the product's rating and comments from other users.

It is very common for users to provide feedback after using a product. Look for those with at least 4 or 5 stars. You're good to go if it falls within your niche.

Demand in the Market

Of course, the product must also be in demand. A product would not exist if there was no demand, but in this case, you must know how strong the demand is. It would be more difficult to sell if it were not widely known.

You'd need to do some research to understand market demand. You can ask fellow affiliates with whom you are familiar, or you can attend group discussions.

This is why, as an affiliate, you must network. You'll gain a better understanding of the market and how it works as you meet and interact with more people.

What if you're a newcomer with fewer networks in this industry? You don't have to worry; you can always look at the market's best-sellers. Without a doubt, it would be the product with the highest user demand.

Sales Letter Credibility

Another aspect of the product to consider is the credibility of the sales letter. If the sales letter does not appeal to you, you should refrain from participating in the product's promotion.

As an affiliate, you understand the value of a well-written sales letter. The product vendors should understand that this is where they will either win or lose you. It would be difficult for their product to convert if they did not prepare a good sales letter.

You should be aware of the essential components of a good sales letter, such as what

What does a good headline resemble? How easy is it to read good copy? Furthermore, the majority of

Most importantly, does it provide enough information about the product?

What you should look for here is whether or not the sales letter has the potential to sell. An appealing sales letter should not necessitate further examination. You would immediately recognize and trust the product.

Promotional Materials Distribution

You should also know whether or not the product vendor provides promotional tools. If they don't, you'll have to do more work. Banners and swipe emails are typically what you should look for in promotional tools.

The majority of product vendors have these ready for affiliates. These tools will greatly simplify your work. Typically, all pertinent information is written in swipe emails. All you have to do is enter your affiliate links (in the provided space) and upload it to your Auto-Responder.

Another **tool you must have in the affiliate** business is the Auto-Responder, which is software that works wonders. The primary function of Auto-Responder is to manage all of your subscribers and segment them into different niches.

The majority of affiliate marketers will use a larger company, such as Aweber or Get Response. For the first 30 days, both offer free or $1 trials.

Upsell

It's best to sell a product with an upsell if you want to earn extra money. When there is an upsell, an affiliate usually receives a 100% commission for the frontend product and a percentage commission for the backend product. The backend product, or upsell, is usually expensive.

Instead of immediately selling high-ticket items, you can commit to selling the frontend product.

If you're unfamiliar with the terms 'frontend' and 'backend,' I'll explain them briefly. A customer is on the frontend product's page when they arrive at a sales page where a product is sold. After making a purchase, they will be directed to another page where another product, known as the backend product, is sold.

Because the backend product is usually more expensive than the frontend product, it is also known as an upsell. A sales funnel is the series of sales pages that customers are directed through.

Having a backend product is an excellent way to increase the profit from a sales funnel. If you sell a product with an upsell, you will also earn a higher commission.

For example, a frontend or low ticket product with a price of $37 will direct them to a backend or upsell page with a price of $77 – this is the basic sales funnel for a product launch.

The sales funnel can be extended with another downsell and then an upsell. This is a completely different realm. So, in order to keep your attention on Affiliate Marketing, I will not go into further detail.

Element that Reoccurs

Receiving recurring payment for commission is extremely rare, but it is also a significant advantage for the affiliate if they find a program that promises recurring commission.

This is typically used for membership sites where each member must pay a monthly fee. As an affiliate, you will be paid a commission for each month they remain a subscriber to the site.

Even though the commission is not as high as that of a high-ticket sale, it still provides a consistent source of income.

Payment is made immediately.

Not long ago, instant payment was unheard of. Affiliates will instead be paid 30 days after a purchase is made. This is due to the fact that customers may request refunds within 30 days. As a result, affiliates will only be compensated when the item sold is non-refundable.

There are now Internet marketplaces that use a system known as 'tentative payment,' in which affiliates receive instant payment. Within 5-7 days, the affiliate will receive 80% of the commission. If a customer requests a refund, the system will make the refund from the remaining 20% of the commission, and the remainder will be paid off after 30 days. Everything is automated.

To avoid conflict, affiliates must always follow the 80/20 rule.

EPC

EPC stands for "Earnings Per Click," and all affiliates must pay close attention to this.

The average earnings for each click that an affiliate sends to the vendor's website is referred to as the EPC. It is an affiliate's conversion rate. It computes for every click. Calculating EPC yields a precise and accurate result for average sales.

The EPC Formula

One does not need to be a mathematician to calculate EPC. It's actually quite simple, and anyone can do it.

The EPC formula is as follows:

EPC = sales / number of clicks

As an example, suppose an affiliate is selling a $100 product. And one product is sold for every 100 clicks directed to the link. The formula is applied as follows:

EPC = sales / number of clicks

$100 divided by 100 clicks equals $1.00.

The EPC costs $1.00.

The higher the EPC, the greater the likelihood that an affiliate will receive a higher commission for the product.

Because the product was priced at $100, the EPC shown above is an example of a high-ticket product's EPC. These products typically have a high EPC value. Selling high -ticket items, on the other hand, can be difficult, and it is recommended that you do so only on occasion.

Furthermore, selling high-ticket items is not advised because few people are interested in them. You are exhausting your list by promoting these products in your emails to your subscribers.

Techniques for Writing Reviews

This chapter will teach you how to write a simple and effective review that generates affiliate commissions, as well as how to create a '1-page affiliate website.' After you've decided on a product to promote, you'll move on to the next step.

What exactly is review writing? Review writing is social proof for a product; it is someone's testimony about the product after using it.

Before we buy something, we usually do some product comparisons and considerations as consumers or customers.

Reviews contain pertinent information. Customers will be more likely to purchase something if they conduct research on review articles online. As a result, excellent review writing can increase sales.

First and foremost, you must obtain review access from the product vendor. There are two methods for obtaining review access:

1. Purchase and

2. Request a review copy from the author.

The first method is the simplest – buy the product and study it. After you've finished evaluating the product, write an article about its advantages and disadvantages.

Tip: You can earn a commission by making the purchase through your own affiliate link. With a 100% commission rate on the product, you spend almost nothing to buy it.

However, you must only buy for the purpose of writing reviews; do not try to defraud the system by selling more than you should.

The second method entails contacting the product vendor and requesting a "review copy" or "full access" to the product. When you join his affiliate program, you will be able to find ways to contact the product vendor. It could be an email address, a Skype ID, or a forum private message.

If you need to contact the product vendor, it is preferable if you can demonstrate yourself as an affiliate capable of generating sales, so that the product vendor will provide you with the'review copy' for free.

There are three ways to demonstrate your credibility to the product vendor; all you need to do is show them:

1. Your previous sales record,

2. Your personal website, or

3. Your email list or website traffic.

The quickest way to establish your credibility is to let the numbers speak for themselves, demonstrating what you are capable of. You may include a file or a screenshot of your previous sales record in the email. This is without a doubt the most convincing evidence you can offer.

Send a link to the product vendor that takes them to your own affiliate site, where they can view the sales page you've created. This is for him to understand how you intend to drive traffic to his website. Keep in mind that you must have the best sales letter prepared and ready to be shown.

Last but not least, disclose the size of your mailing list or the volume of traffic to your website. The number of mailing lists indicates the maximum amount of traffic that you can send to his site; a larger list would be advantageous.

Here is an example of an email; you can see how it should be done:

Hello [vendor],

My name is [your name], and I've just asked for permission to promote your newest product, close-up.

I was wondering if I could have access to your most recent offer? I don't need full product access; a review copy will suffice. This is so that I can provide an unbiased review of your newest product.

I currently have over 75,000 email subscribers to whom I will send your offer. I'll also be handing out my own Bonus offers to anyone who purchases through my link.

I'm hoping to hear from you soon!

[Your surname]

The size of the mailing list is shown in this email to persuade the product vendor to grant access to the product. Furthermore, it demonstrates the effort you'll put forth to convert traffic to the vendor's site by dispensing your own Bonus offers.

What is mentioned in the email may apply to someone who has been in the affiliate business for a long time, but what if you are a newbie with no past sales record and a small mailing list?

In this case, I strongly advise you to purchase the product rather than obtaining free access to it. You can, however, send an email to the product vendor and request a discount.

Here's an example of an email to request the discount:

> *Hello [vendor],*
>
>
> *My name is [your name], and I've just asked for permission to promote your newest product, Close-up.*
>
> *I am new to affiliate marketing and have recently launched a new website*

with the goal of promoting your offer. I was wondering if you could provide me with review access to your product?

I would appreciate it if you could provide me with some sort of discount, as my main goal is to write an honest review of your product before putting in my marketing efforts to promote your offer.

I'm hoping to hear from you soon!

[Your surname]

After you have purchased or obtained access to the product, you can begin planning how you will write the review for the product.

Techniques for Writing Reviews

As previously stated, a good review article can increase conversion rates and thus sales. From here on out, I'll walk you through the process of writing a good review article step by step.

To begin, try to limit your review writing to 300-500 words. A review article should be direct and precise. Show them only the information they need to know, such as the pros and cons or a testimonial from someone who has used the product. Anything more than 500 words will be too long for your readers' attention span.

Write in a conversational tone – a message from me to you. You are not required to be formal. Make it more personal and friendly, because the point of writing a review is to tell them how you feel about a product.

There are only two things you need to focus on when writing a review: the product's pros and cons. Remember to be concise and to the point; do not exaggerate the benefits of the product and skip over the disadvantages in order to increase sales.

Insert a product photo or screenshots from various angles into your review article so that readers can see exactly how the product will look with the visual aids you've provided.

Fact 1: Add a 5-star rating system to your article as well. This is very common in review writing nowadays. It gives readers a rough idea of how they would rate if they were not the reading type.

Fact 2:: If the product you're promoting requires demonstration, include a video in your review or upload it to YouTube. While demonstrating in the video, explain the product's features and functions.

Fact 3:: Include the benefits and drawbacks in the form comparison chart. In the form of a chart, it is easier to read and compare. Furthermore, if you are selling a physical product, look for another similar product to create a comparison chart.

Create Your Own Review Article Website

After you've completed your review writing, you'll need a platform to upload your review article — a review article website. With the assistance of various software, creating your own website is no longer as difficult as it once was.

If you follow these three simple steps, you will be able to quickly and effectively set up your own review article site.

1. Install WordPress,

2. Purchase a Domain Name and then

3. Use your own server to host it.

Your website will be up and running in almost no time. Let's get started with the steps.

Step 1: Install WordPress

WordPress is a piece of software that allows you to create your own website in a few simple steps.

I'd like to tell you exactly how to set up

WordPress, but I don't want to divert your attention away from Affiliate Marketing. To summarize, you can go to WordPress.org and find a short documentation on how to set up WordPress and use it to start your own website. You can also go to YouTube and look for some simple tutorials on it.

This is easy to do, and best of all, it is free! However, there are premium packages for business use; if you want more features in WordPress and don't mind spending more money, go for the paid version.

Following that, you can begin editing your own website. WordPress is extremely simple to use, and you don't need to understand HTML to make changes to your content. All you need to do is some basic drag-and-drop design work, and you'll be able to publish it once you're finished.

You can create multiple websites using a single account. You can also delete the website at any time. The SEO checking system built into the software is one of the highlighted features that I believe is extremely important in WordPress.

There is an indicator that allows you to check the SEO score of your article. If your article fails the SEO test, you can always change the keywords in the headline, meta-descriptions, and content. You can always make minor changes. The SEO indicator will show you which parts of your website are less SEO-friendly.

Step 2: Purchase a Domain Name

You cannot create a website by utilizing other servers such as WordPress or Blogger. Customers will not trust your website if it ends in ".wordpress.com." As a result, purchasing your own domain name is required.

NameCheap.com is one of the sites you can visit. There are additional domains.

Of course, there are registrars, but this is

the one that comes highly recommended.

Once there, you can check the availability of any given name. Before we get there, there's one thing you should do: come up with a domain name.

The key here is to make it searchable, clear, and simple to comprehend.

You can combine any words and phrases related to the product into a single word. As an example:

Here are some examples of common domain names:

   i.   **Special.com**
  ii.   **Review.com**
 iii.   **Bonus.com**

All of these are optional domain names that I frequently use.

Make at least ten of these domain names so that you have more options. After deciding on the best available name, you can purchase and register it.

Following that, you'll **require a website server**.

Step 3: Use Your Own Server to Host

Following that, you'll require a host to upload your website. Here are two dependable hosts:

1. **Hostgator.com** – the most popular option among internet marketers

2. **BlueHost.com** – yet another highly regarded and dependable hosting service.

This is the stage at which you can obtain an official.com website, such as whatever.com. Don't use a free blog like whatever.wordpress.com because people take a.com website more seriously than a.wordpress.com or.blogspot.com.

It almost sounds like another blog. It does not exude professionalism.

Here is the three-step formula for creating a website. No more tinkering with HTML codes to create a website! If you are not interested in using WordPress to create your website, HTML and Dreamweaver are two other options.

Creating an Affiliate Business Empire

In this chapter, I'll show you **how to create a simple website** to grow your mailing list, how to write simple, fast, and effective promotional emails, and how to follow up with your subscribers.

The mailing list is your most valuable asset in building your affiliate business empire. The larger your list, the more profit you can make. However, most marketers frequently overlook an important step, which is to direct traffic to their own landing page first.

It is strongly advised that you do not send traffic directly to the vendor's page via your affiliate link. If you do this, 96-98 percent of the traffic will be lost. The vendor will receive all of the emails, while you will only receive a few commissions. Why should you settle for less when you can have more?

You lose money if you paid for traffic but the vendor's sales letter does not sell! To solve this and make it a win-win situation for both you and the vendor, you direct your traffic to your own landing page first, where you collect their email address.

A landing page is a page where visitors can enter their name and email address. It is straightforward and typically minimal, with few designs. Please do not include any sales letters here. Your call to action should be included in the promotional emails, which I will discuss further in this chapter.

The following is the format of a landing page:

1.   introductory phrase

2.   The sub-headline

3.   The free report's graphics

4. Sign-up form

5. Free report download button

Here's an example of how a landing page should appear:

The headline on your landing page should be in either dark red or black, with dark red being preferred. The headline is usually a teaser for the visitor to take action. Tahoma, Arial Black, and Helvetica are the most commonly used fonts for headlines.

In this case, the headline is "Grab This

Report & Brand Yourself As An Expert In The Hottest Wave In Social Media" in dark red with a call to action!

Tip: If you look closely, you'll notice that the first letter of each word is capitalized. This has been shown to be easier for visitors to read, increasing the likelihood of visitors finishing the headline.

It is then followed by the product's graphics. As you are aware, graphics are extremely important in a website. Put yourself in the visitor's shoes: Would you want to read a page full of words? Or do you prefer a website with visual aids in the middle? I don't need a crystal ball to tell me that the latter is the correct answer.

The big red arrow pointing down to the opt-in form is the next element at the bottom of the graphics. This large red arrow has been shown to be eye-catching. The first thing your visitor will notice is the big arrow, followed by the opt-in form where they can enter their email address.

The most important opt-in form is below the red arrow, with an orange or yellow sign -up button. This orange and yellow button has been shown to increase conversion rates.

This is the primary goal of a landing page; the other elements serve as a call to action to entice visitors to enter their email addresses and join your mailing list.

When your mailing list grows in size, I'm not talking about a few hundreds here, but thousands or even millions, you'll need software to manage it for you! It's referred to as Auto-Responder.

What Auto-Responder can do for you is critical. It simplifies your job. You can manage your email list with just a few clicks.

Here are some of the **basic functions of the Auto-Responder**

1. Follow-up via auto-responder

2. Rate of email deliverability

3. Sign-up forms that have been completed for you

4. Prepared-for-you email newsletters

5. Emails generated automatically from your blog posts

6. Editor with drag and drop

7. Subscriber management

8. Subscriber segmentation

9. Tracking of email marketing

These are the software's fundamental features. The software allows you to automate tasks. *GetResponse.com* and Aweber.com are two low-cost and effective Auto-Responders. You can get these amazing features for a low monthly fee.

Following the opt-in of an email address on the landing page, direct traffic to the vendor's page via your affiliate link. It is critical that you direct them to your affiliate link. If you do not do this, even if they buy the product, you will not receive the commission.

That is the first option; the second is to redirect the traffic to your bonus or review page. This is the most recommended method because the bonuses and review pages you have shown them can help you build your credibility. As a result, you retain your subscribers.

If you are not a reliable source, your subscribers will eventually stop following you and will click the unsubscribe button.

Example of Affiliate Marketing

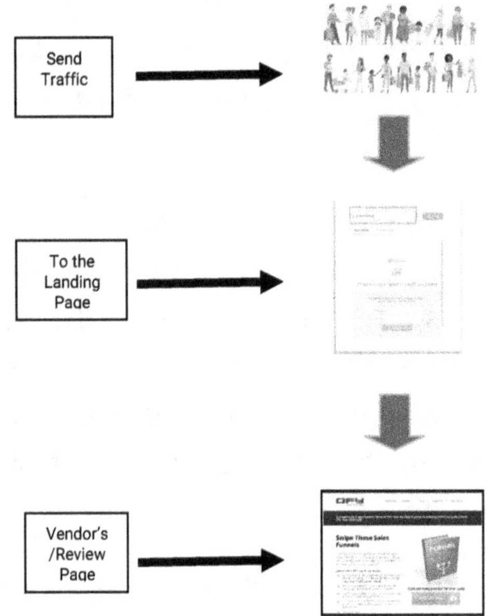

This is exactly how it should be. Step 1 is to direct traffic to the landing page first, followed by the vendor's page or your bonus or review page.

A bonus page is essentially an extra page where you give away one or more of your products as a thank you for subscribing to your newsletters. A review page, on the other hand, is where you write reviews about the product you are promoting at the time.

To write a product review article, you must first understand and be familiar with the product. You can either obtain review access from the vendor or purchase it from the vendor, using your affiliate link, as described in the Review Writing Technique chapter.

Here's an example of a review page I created for you.

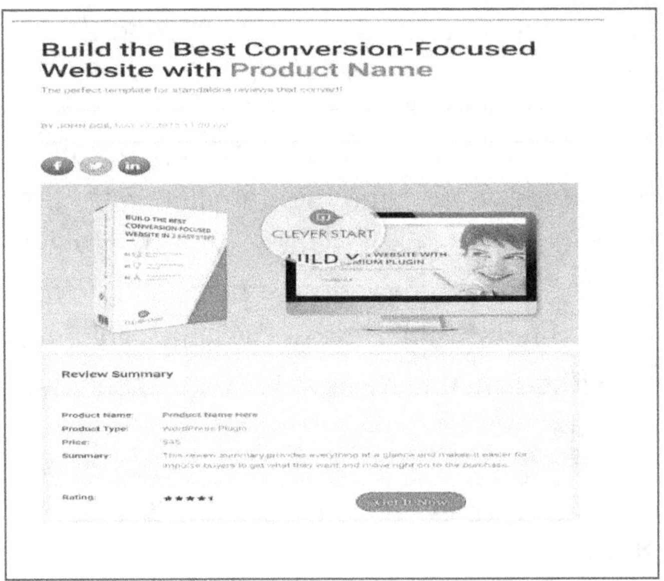

As promised earlier, I will now show you how to write follow-up emails. An email consists of only two parts: the headline and the body. The subject line of the email is the headline that will appear in the subscribers' inboxes.

The headline is the most important part because it determines whether your email will be read by subscribers or deleted without being read by them.

So, what is the most important thing to remember when writing a headline that entices people to open it?

The first method is to employ numbers, statistics, or the scarcity factor. When there are numbers or statistics that prove you are not a scam, the likelihood that people will click on it and see what's inside increases.

Scarcity factor is similar to the 'limited sales' technique; it is a common marketing technique used to make people feel compelled to buy something because supplies are limited.

For example, a headline that says "Bonus!" Only 50... or something like that. People adore the phrase "limited edition." They'd jump into action more quickly.

Reasons why I despise MLM, for example... or Is this the last piece of software you'll ever need? They won't know what this email is about until they click to open it.

Hint 1: Use sentence case in your headline to make it easier to read. Contrast these two:

my review for optimize press

My Review For Optimize Press

Which is the easier to read? The second one, of course.

Hint 2: Limit your subject line to 35-50 characters. The reason you should keep your subject line characters to a minimum is that the mailbox will only display the first 50 characters. Anything longer than this will be omitted.

If your subject line is too long, it will be cut off in the middle of the sentence.

The body of an email is the second section. The key for the body is to be straightforward and precise. You don't need to write a long email if there are only one or two key points you want them to know.

If the email is too long, they might not be able to read it all.

Don't squander sales opportunities because of lengthy emails. Keep it brief (200-300 words) and to the point. In the email, get right to the "what's in it for me" and call to action.

After the call to action, always include a URL link to the same site.

The ideal way to include a URL link in an email is three times – at the beginning, middle, and end.

Too many calls to action leave a negative impression on them; three is the ideal number. The URL can point to your affiliate link, bonus page, or review page. The most recommended method, as previously stated, is to link to the bonus or review page.

Hint: Keep your email's body to 55 characters per line. Why? People prefer shorter line lengths because they find them easier to read. If you were to read an email from beginning to end, would it be easier to read half of the page and then move on to the next line?

This is a tried-and-true method that has proven to be effective in email marketing.

How frequently should you send follow-up emails to your subscribers now? My response to you will be at least four follow-up emails, with a one-email-per-day interval.

The emails you'll be sending should look like this:

The first day: The Initial Promotional Email

Second day: Email Reminder

Third day: Email Q&A

The last day : Email with the Last Call

<u>Hint 1</u>:Remember to send all of these emails to your subscribers via Auto-Responder. Auto-Responder is a small hack

that allows you to send emails on the day you want them to be sent automatically.

Hint 2: Use a link tracker or link-cloaker to keep track of who is clicking on the links in your emails. You can improve your email writing skills by running split tests on the elements of your emails.

Hint 3: Change one element at a time to see which one drives the most traffic to the website to which you've linked. No need to be concerned about this; it is one of the services provided by Auto-Responder.

What if your link is complicated and lengthy? People are unlikely to click on long links with indecipherable words if they suspect it is a virus link. YoURLs.org can help you simplify your link and get more clicks with a much simpler link! The best part is that it is completely free!

Use Pay-Per-Click to Drive Traffic

Pay-per-click advertising is one method of

generating traffic to your website. The advertiser must pay for each click on that specific link under this arrangement.

This advertising service is provided by Google and Bing, the two largest search engines.

How Does It Work?

With Google, you will use a program called Google Adwords, which allows you to bid on the most searched keyword that is relevant to your product. If you win the bid, your website will be prioritized in Google search results.

The higher the bidding price, the higher the search for the keyword.

The key word here, however, is'relevance.' Google has an excellent customer relationship, and they go out of their way to protect it. When a bidder submits a bid for a keyword, Google will dispatch editors to assess the relevance of the website's service or product to the keyword.

If there is no relevancy, the bidding is null and void. This is how Google responds to false advertising. If this method is used, always prioritize relevancy over popularity of a specific keyword.

You pay the ad space provider using a pay-per-click system, which requires you to pay for each click you receive.

How to Make Use of **Google** AdWords

1. Open an AdWords account

First and foremost, you must create a Google Adwords account. If you already have a Gmail account, you won't have to enter any of the information that you've already entered for your Gmail account. All you need is your email address and password to get started.

You don't have to worry about payment with Google Adwords just yet. Registration is completely free.

2. Select keywords

This is where you will have to compete with millions of other users who are most likely competing for the same keywords as you. Find the keywords that are most relevant to your products so that customers can find you.

3. Create a daily budget.

Finally, based on your financial plan, create a daily budget. If the average cost-per-click for that particular keyword is ten cents, and you want to bid for 100 clicks per day, your daily budget will be ten cents multiplied by 100, for a total of ten dollars per day. The starting bid for different keywords may differ. Of course, after some time of testing traffic and keywords, you can change your daily budget from Google Adwords at any time to increase the number of clicks to your site.

Instead of keywords, use key phrases.

Gaining popularity through keyword searches is great, but if you could put yourself in the shoes of the customer, you would know that they would not search for keywords. Instead, they would search using phrases.

Customers who want to learn about Facebook advertising, for example, would type "How do I advertise on Facebook" into the search box. This is a common mistake made by people who want to use Google Adwords to promote their product.

Keeping a Record of Your Clicks

The Google Adwords Dimension Tab is a feature in Google Adwords that allows users to track the number of clicks they receive. The Dimension Tab's primary function is to analyze the amount of traffic and clicks generated by Google Adwords.

First, the Dimension Tab examines the clicks in terms of time. They analyze and present to you statistics ranging from an hour to a year. This way, you'll know when it's best to place your ads.

For example, if the results show that Saturday has the lowest performance, you may want to pause your ads on weekends. On weekdays, you can save some money for a better bid.

Second, Dimension Tabs analyzes your ad's geographic location. You can use this feature to determine which parts of the world your ad performs best in. You can sort these statistics by conversions, countries, states, and other criteria. This is done so that you can determine who your target audience is.

The search terms are the third feature in this case. The search terms analysis enables you to learn about all of the other search terms that triggered your ads from multiple perspectives.

At this point in the search terms analysis chart, you can see what kind of keywords users use in search engines to find your site. You might find some useful keywords here for future use, or if some irrelevant terms have made their way in, you can remove them right away.

Use Solo Ads to Drive Traffic

In this chapter, I will introduce you to one of the methods for increasing traffic to your website solo ads. First and foremost, why use solo ads when there are so many other options?

This is why:

Reason #1: It is the quickest and most effective.

For starters, buying solo ads from other vendors is the quickest and most effective way to generate traffic to your site, because you don't have a large mailing list to send promotional emails to.

So, in order to expand your mailing list, you must purchase solo ads from other vendors.

Furthermore, you have control over how much you spend. The total amount you must pay is determined by how much traffic the vendors sent to your page, which is referred to as "pay per click." I'll go into more detail about pay per click later.

Reason #2 Targeted Leads

You will get all targeted leads to your site by purchasing solo ads from vendors in the same niche as yours. They send traffic to your site that is interested in your offer, rather than traffic from other niches that are not your target and are unlikely to make any purchases.

Another advantage of purchasing solo ads is that you can expand your mailing list. When the vendor-directed leads who come to your site make a purchase, you can collect their email addresses via the landing page.

Reason #3: Instant gratification and a high conversion rate

The results of the conversion rate can be seen almost immediately, which is the best part about purchasing solo ads. The vendor from whom you purchase solo ads will immediately send the solo ads email to their subscribers in order to promote your affiliate link.

This is why you don't have to wait for a long time for traffic to your website.

Here are the three reasons why I chose to introduce solo ads over all other methods of generating traffic.

However, most marketers overlook the fact that solo ad emails are only used to PRESELL. Instead, they put the sales page in their solo ad emails, which is why so many of them are unable to grow their mailing list by purchasing solo ads.

Of course, seeing the solo ad emails comes first in the sequence of how solo ads should work. Second, they are directed to a landing page where they can enter their email address, and finally, they are directed to the sales page for the promoted product.

This is how the sequence should go; don't include any sales-related messages in your solo ad email; instead, include a message about the free report they can download if they opt in their email address today. The messages in the solo ad and the landing page must be consistent so that the readers understand.

Here's an example of a landing page that you can revise:

As you can see, it begins with a simple but action-oriented headline about the free report your subscribers will receive after opting in with their email address, followed by a call to action to fill out the box below with a big red arrow pointing down and an orange call to action button.

Tip: If you only ask for their email address with a single opt-in, your conversion rate will be higher. Some marketers will request double opt-in, but this will not increase conversion rates.

Because this is the most common format for a landing page, your solo ad email should mention the free report rather than the product you're promoting. Allow the vendor to sell through the sales page. It is your responsibility to direct traffic to their website.

How to Create a Solo Ad
A solo ad email does not have to be overly

complicated. It must be simple so that readers can understand it. The following is the basic and effective format for a solo ad:

1. **Brief and precise** – no more than 200 words and no more than 55 characters per line

2. **Three Urls** pointing to the same website – beginning, middle, and end

This should also be the basic format of a solo ad email.

Tip: Make a semi-blind offer in which you only reveal half of the information about the offer. This is one of the cliffhanger techniques used to pique their interest in learning more about the next offer you'll make to them.

The solo ad should be written as follows:

Hello, [[firstname]].

You owe it to yourself to see this if you are
 and :

[[THIS LINK GOES HERE]]

Here's how to .

Click here to learn more right now:

[[THIS LINK GOES HERE]]

YOUR BRAND NAME

P.S. You can join right now for free. Here it is once more:

[[THIS LINK GOES HERE]]

As previously stated, you should direct traffic to your landing page first! To collect email addresses from subscribers in order to grow the mailing list, because the size of the mailing list is an affiliate's most valuable asset, do not send the vendor sales copy first.

The first priority should be to build your own mailing list.

How to Keep Track of Conversions

Tracking the conversion rate to the site is also essential because you'll need to know how many clicks you've sent to the vendor's page. Google Analytics and Link Tracker Tool are recommended tools.

Google Analytics is a free service offered by Google; you can find it using the Google search engine and sign up for it for free! However, there are several link tracker tools available online that you can buy if you need more features.

Reliable Sources for Solo Ad Vendors

Go to SoloChecker.com and look for a package that fits your budget. You'll need to know how many clicks you want to buy from the vendor – 50, 100, 200, 500, or 1000.

This is one of the more reliable options, or you can simply search Google for'solo ad' or 'email advertising' plus your 'niche name'.

If you can, contact a few solo ad vendors and gather all of the necessary information; the "Questions to Ask" section has already been completed for you; I'll reveal it to you later.

The purpose of asking them these questions is for comparison purposes, such as comparing price, mailing list size, reliability, and so on.

The number of clicks you purchased is the amount of traffic you will receive; this way, you will know exactly what you will receive. In the worst-case scenario, the number of clicks sent by the vendor is not equal to the number of clicks you purchased from him.

This is another reason **why tracking is essential**: you need to know your phone number in case something goes wrong. To avoid a conflict, you must first discuss the terms and conditions with the vendor.

The following are the "Questions to Ask":

1. What is the size of your email list?

2. How do you obtain my leads?

3. How many clicks can you generate?

4. Can you make me an appropriate offer?

5. How 'ancient' is your list?

These are the most frequently asked questions to ensure that the vendor with whom you are collaborating is trustworthy. The final question is to ensure that the mailing list is up to date; if the mailing list is too old, you may want to reconsider doing business with him.

The most important aspect of dealing with the vendor is determining how much you should spend. The cost per click will be between $0.20 and $0.50. For example, the first option of 100 clicks for $40 will result in a cost of $0.40 per click. Do the math and figure out how much you're paying for clicks.

For starters, you should start small with

100 clicks. Always remember to keep track of the number of clicks to your site.

Using Blogs to Make Money

There are numerous benefits to writing a blog. It allows you to not only express and share your ideas and opinions, but it can also be used to sell your products. This is an important aspect of your business as an affiliate marketer.

Why Have a Blog?

As an affiliate marketer, you must establish a rapport with your customers. One of the benefits of this is that you can form relationships with your customers. Customers must be assured that they are not purchasing products from a robot on the Internet. Allow them to see a side of you that is more than just an affiliate marketer.

This 'human touch' goes a long way toward establishing trust between you and your customers. Use your blog to express your thoughts, ideas, or simply to share pictures of your travels and adventures. Some may scoff at the idea, but it is done to remind customers that you are just like them.

All affiliates should have personality, or, more accurately, a friendly and approachable personality. It may not be good for business if you go into this venture without a personality, hiding behind a name and a picture.

Customers want to see the other side of you, the one that isn't focused on selling products.

What Should You Do With Your Blog?

As previously stated, simply write about anything related to your business and the products you sell. It's perfectly fine to deviate from that every now and then to discuss your interests in a couple of posts.

The key to having a large number of readers and followers on your blog is to have high-quality content. However, you must also interact with the readers. You must entertain them when they read something you've written and want to comment on that specific topic. They value the fact that you read and value their ideas and opinions.

You can also learn something new about yourself by reading and responding to the comments.

Develop Relationships With Other Bloggers

As you are aware, networking is essential in business. It is also critical to network with other bloggers in the same niche.

You can interact with other bloggers by leaving comments, liking their posts, or sharing them on social media platforms like Facebook and Twitter. You should also interact with them on social media by adding them to your Facebook friends list or following them on Twitter.

When you promote their posts, they may share yours in return. You will gain new unique readers as a result of their following. You can also get advice and pointers from them if they are experts in the same field as you.

There are numerous advantages to networking, and there is no reason to avoid it. Another great reason to network with other bloggers is to write a guest post on their blog.

Blogging as a Guest

This is one of the most effective ways to attract new readers to your blog. Guest blogging is simply writing a post for someone else's blog and having them do the same for you.

To do so, you must first find a blog that discusses the same topic as your own. It's best to find a blog with nearly the same number of readers and followers as you.

Then, as previously mentioned, you must interact with them via social media or commenting. Then, pitch the idea of guest blogging to them.

What is the point of doing this? This allows you to get new traffic from the same niche without having to go to other unfamiliar places on the Internet. By writing a guest post, you gain access to the attention of the other blogger's readers and followers. If they like what you write, they will visit your blog as well.

Finding a blog with the same niche and topic as yours is important because you know your readers and followers are interested in that specific niche. As a result, the chances are that they will enjoy your blog as well. And keep in mind that these readers are also your target audience. You gain new exposure to an untapped target audience by guest blogging.

Typically, a guest-blogging arrangement does not necessitate any monetary investment. If you have a large number of readers and followers, the other blogger may be willing to do this guest posting for free. This is yet another non-monetary form of advertising.

Guest Posting on a Blog

It is entirely up to you to write a blog post. You are free to choose your own path, but here are some suggestions based on popular posts.

a. Include Images

Incorporate images into your posts. Communication has become more visual than ever before. Additionally, having images is a surefire way to capture the attention of a blog reader.

Visual aid is required if your blog post is a tutorial or guide. This is done so that your readers can better understand your post.

You will need images to accompany your writing, especially if it involves numbers. You can share images such as charts, graphs, and so on.

b. Add Hyperlinks

When making a point and needing evidence to back it up in a post, you must quote the source of that information. This can be included as a hyperlink in the post itself. You don't have to worry about readers getting distracted from the post because that rarely happens.

They rarely click on these hyperlinks, but having them available is still a good idea.

c. Make Your Blog Visible and Accessible

Include a link to your own blog at the end

of the post (or at the beginning, if you prefer) so that readers can find more of your writings.

People are wary of naked links, so you must disguise them with a hyperlink. Make your blog's link as visible and accessible as possible. This will entice them to pay a visit to your blog.

The Most Common Mistakes Internet Marketers Made

Because of the rapid advancement of technology, an increasing number of startups have emerged; internet marketing is no longer novel to us. However, not every Internet marketer will make it to the end because they do not know how to do it correctly.

As a result, if you see a flat movement in your conversion rates and sales rate despite doing everything possible to send the swipe emails to your subscribers, you have yet to determine which aspect of your marketing you did incorrectly.

If you find yourself in the same situation, you will be losing money if you haven't read this section of the book. I'm going to tell you about some common mistakes you may have made that you weren't aware of.

Spam

This is one of the most common mistakes that an Internet marketer, particularly a newbie, makes but fails to recognize. This is a common misconception: "The more emails I send, the more sales I will make." This is a mistake that you must avoid when developing your email marketing strategies.

Put yourself in your subscribers' shoes. You wouldn't want to receive emails every day from someone trying to sell you something.

You can avoid this by incorporating a double opt-in system into your landing page. Double opt-in requires the prospect to enter their email address twice to confirm their subscription, so it is a double confirmation act that they are giving you permission to send them your newsletters.

True, you may lose some subscribers as a result of the double opt-in system, but consider this from another perspective: those who double confirm their consent and subscribe to your newsletters are the serious prospects who would consider your offer.

In comparison to obtaining a large number of'subscribers,' having a list of'serious buyers' would be advantageous.

A Little Hint for you: Make sure the system for unsubscribing to your newsletters works properly. Even though it is preferable to keep your list, it is their right to opt-out and choose what types of emails they want to receive.

Using the Wrong Words

If used correctly, the art of words can be

very powerful. This is a difficult lesson for every Internet marketer to learn, but if you can master it, you can easily earn the title of super affiliate.

To meet the needs of internet users, the way of writing emails and sales letters has evolved numerous times over the years. Words that were effective a few years ago will no longer be able to capture the attention of users.

To master the art of words, you must first understand your prospects' needs. Prospect research may require a significant amount of time and effort, but it will greatly assist you in fine-tuning the way you write to them. This minor change could result in massive sales for you, but you won't know until you try it.

A split test is one method for improving word choice. To begin, divide your mailing list in half. Every time you send an email to your subscribers, change one element of it. Send the first edition of your email to half of the recipients, and the second edition to the other half.

You can monitor the conversion rate by using a tracking system service available on the internet. This way, you can continuously improve your email marketing. You can change the subject line, the opening call to action, or the closing call to action. Remember to only change one element at a time in order to keep track of which element affects the conversion rate.

Because the Internet business is an ever-changing platform, it is recommended to do this on a regular basis. The way things were done as recently as last year may no longer be applicable now.

Attract the Wrong Kind of Traffic

This is especially important for newbies who don't know how to drive targeted traffic to their landing pages. When you direct the wrong people to your landing page, it will have an effect on your subscriber list as well. It may appear that you are gaining a large number of subscribers, but these are not the targeted subscribers that you require.

They want instant gratification but go about it in the wrong way, such as generating traffic from different niches. This is not the best way to generate traffic; all you'll get is more subscribers but no sales.

or beginners, be patient and begin with a small amount at first. There are ways to get immediate results while also increasing your sales, such as buying solo ads or doing ad swaps with other Internet marketers.

After a few solo ad purchases, you can begin doing ad swaps with a larger list. Growing your mailing list should be the most important task for any Internet marketer.

Despite all of these techniques, some

Internet marketers continue to do this incorrectly. Going to the incorrect site and generating incorrect traffic to the landing page

As a result, they were unable to sustain and survive in business.

Couldn't Find the Demand

A product or service demanded by consumers differs from the product or service desired by consumers. While demands are something that consumers require, a product or service that consumers want is simply something they want − not something they require.

In comparison to a consumer's immediate and immediate desire, a product that can fulfill a consumer's long-term needs is clearly a better choice. Nonetheless, some marketers only see the business's short-term objectives.

They couldn't figure out which products are evergreen and will last longer in the market.

Aside from that, they have occasionally forgotten to ensure that the product is a proven seller. A product that is desired by the public but is unable to sell is no different than a product that should not be sold.

Before you decide to sell that particular product, do some research on the credibility of the product vendor, the quality of the product, the sales page, the sales funnels, and so much more.

So, even if it is a product that consumers want, make sure it is a proven seller.

Couldn't Find the Correct Product

This is a major blunder that could jeopardize your credibility and sales. As previously stated, conduct product research to determine the best product to promote.

To begin with, this is an unavoidable act, especially for newcomers. Alternatively, this is the first time you promote the vendor's products.

Choose vendors who are solely concerned with lead generation. This type of product is usually not of high quality because the focus is solely on growing the mailing list and not on the product's quality.

If you promote a low-quality product and lead your subscribers to subscribe to someone who will spam them via email marketing, your credibility will be ruined. Worst-case scenario, your newsletter subscribers unsubscribe.

So, be certain of the type of product you are promoting.

Keeping Your Affiliate Commission Safe

Thanks to the astonishing rate at which internet technologies are evolving, we now have a plethora of advantages that make our lives far more convenient than in the past. However, we must consider not only the advantages of the Internet, but also its disadvantages.

Given the lucrative commissions that being an affiliate can bring to Internet marketers, thieves will not pass up the opportunity to steal from you as well!

At the same time that you are earning passive income through the affiliate program, you should be on the lookout for thieves. An Internet business owner should be aware of this and install anti-theft software in their system. This is done to keep your affiliate commission from being targeted.

Here are some things you can do to protect your company and prevent this from happening:

Refresh the Metadata

It is a method of instructing a web browser

to automatically refresh a specific page after a set amount of time. This step can help to reduce commission bypassing without notice, as well as commission hijacking from an unwelcome thief.

This, however, necessitates a basic understanding of HTML scripting. Even a novice script writer can do this by changing the HTML scripts in their browser. Simply searching for the command to enter into the script will suffice.

Despite the benefits that Meta refresh can provide, there is one issue that Meta refresh may bring to your site. Some search engines dislike Meta refreshes because some site owners have used them for nefarious purposes. If you decide to use this method, proceed with caution.

Service for Redirecting URLs

The URL redirecting service, also known as URL forwarding, allows you to make a web page available under more than one URL address. When someone tries to open the redirected website, the website with a different URL is opened.

You can find this service for free on the internet, or if you are not on a tight budget, you can purchase a domain name for each affiliate program that you join. This is a method that reduces the chances of the same URL appearing too frequently, lowering the chances of being targeted by a commission thief.

Ad Tracking Service on the Internet

You can use this service to determine which website directed the prospect to your affiliate page. Because it records the entire advertising campaign, this is a common service for Internet marketers to study which advertising method is the best.

However, as an affiliate, you can use this service to determine where visitors to your site came from. If there is a suspicious source, you can quickly identify and resolve the issue before it causes you any harm.

Scripts for Ad Tracking

If you don't want to use online services, you can use ad tracking scripts instead. However, you must be familiar with HTML scripts in order to do so.

You can find some useful scripts on the internet that will notify you if they discover any suspicious sources that lead to your site. Knowing how to write ad tracking scripts has the advantage of making tracking work easier because the system is automated.

You can reduce the risk by hiding your affiliate link from the thief using the ad tracking script.

Redirection in JavaScript

This is another script that allows you to redirect your visitors from the first site they visit to another. When exactly will someone require the JavaScript redirect? It is the time when you must transfer your website to a new domain name.

You can place the JavaScript redirect in your old domain name to notify visitors that your site has moved to a new domain name. There will be a new link that will take them to the new website.

You can save your redirect URL in a custom field and set the type to hidden. This way, your redirected URL will be hidden; only those with permission will be able to see it. As a result, commission thief can be reduced as well.

Conclusion

If you know the right techniques, affiliate marketing can provide you with numerous opportunities and a lucrative passive income. Furthermore, the flexible time that allows an affiliate to work from home is another appealing feature that entices people to join the bandwagon.

It is largely up to you whether your affiliate business succeeds or fails. You can start your own affiliate business with more knowledge than other affiliate marketers who have navigated the same waters now that you understand how an affiliate business works.

Keep in mind not to give up so easily. Here's to your business's success!